HOW TO GET STRAIGHT A's GUARANTEED!

HOW TO GET STRAIGHT A's GUARANTEED!

Six Secrets to Success in College

Lyman Rose

CFI
Springville, Utah

ISBN 13: 978-1-59955-092-3

Published by CFI, an imprint of Cedar Fort, Inc., 2373 W. 700 S., Springville, UT, 84663
Distributed by Cedar Fort, Inc., www.cedarfort.com

LIBRARY OF CONGRESS CATALOGING-IN-PUBLICATION DATA

Rose, Lyman Hinckley, 1958–
How to get straight A's, guaranteed! / Lyman Rose.
p. cm.
Includes bibliographical references.
ISBN 978-1-59955-092-3
1. Study skills—United States. 2. College student orientation—United States. I. Title.

LB2395.R748 2008
378.1'70281—dc22

2008000510

Cover design by Jeremy Beal
Cover design © 2008 by Lyle Mortimer
Edited and typeset by Christy M. Bigelow

Printed in the United States of America

10 9 8 7 6 5 4 3 2 1

Printed on acid-free paper

Contents

Introduction

If you follow the plan in this book and use all of the tools, it will be almost impossible to avoid getting straight A's. I really wish that I had had this information when I was going to school. It would have made a huge difference. I did okay, but I really could have received straight A's if I had followed these simple rules I'm about to give you.

My first semester at college was very difficult. I followed my parents' advice and went to see a counselor in order to set up my class schedule. When I left his office and signed up for the classes we talked about, I became confused. It was during the summer term, which was really a half semester, so the classes were twice as long as normal.

My first class was scheduled from 7:00 AM

to 9:00 AM, but I had another class that was scheduled from 8:00 AM to 10:00 AM. Of course I had another class scheduled from 9:00 AM to 11:00 AM, and so on. My entire day went like that, five days a week. My schedule was full with double classes from 7:00 AM to 7:00 PM. I had to leave every class halfway through in order to get to the next class.

I couldn't understand how the other students could stay in class for the last hour when I had to go. On top of that, I was trying to do homework and trying to find out what went on during the last hour of the classes. I had so little time to eat that I would just buy a pack of hot dogs for each day and eat two for breakfast, three for lunch, and three for dinner. It was all I had time to prepare! My roommates began to call me Hot Dog. (They still do.)

I was frustrated and felt like I could not continue doing college the way I was doing it. Finally I called my mother and told her that I needed to come home. I told her that although I had done fairly well in high school, I could not take the rigors of college. I may have even been in tears when we spoke. Once again, she suggested that I go to see the counselor and ask him how the other students were able to stay through an entire class when I had to leave halfway through in order to get to my next class.

I followed her advice and went to see my counselor. When I sat down, he could tell I was distraught. He asked me what was wrong, and when I began to explain, he said there must be a problem. He asked his secretary to get a copy of my schedule. When she brought it in, my counselor took a long look at it and then sat way back in his chair and started to laugh. He laughed and laughed, much to my amazement. He laughed so much I almost smiled through my downtrodden face.

Finally he told me that I was taking sixty credit hours when full time for the summer term was nine. He said that when he had told me what classes to take, he was outlining the classes for my entire associate's program for the next two years. I had not realized that I was only supposed to sign up for nine hours that term.

He asked his secretary to come in, and he gave her adjustments to make in my schedule. He then called the registration department to see how my schedule could have possibly cleared their system. With the changes in my schedule bringing me down to just nine hours, I felt like a huge weight had been lifted off me, and I was able to sit through the entire class period for all of my classes. With such a "light" schedule, I was able to do very well.

I hope that you don't have to go through that kind of an ordeal in order to make you feel better about your college experience. If you put the ideas in this book to work for you, your college experience will be great from the start. There are not many more desperate feelings than going to a class unprepared and hoping that the professor doesn't call on you. On the opposite end of things, there aren't many better feelings than going to that same class totally prepared and hoping that the professor does call on you.

This plan is basic, simple, and easy to implement, but it will obviously take some effort on your part. I am not going to simply tell you to study. What I will do is outline a process that is proven, effective, and that will get you the grades you want.

If you are intelligent enough to have been accepted into a college, you are intelligent enough to implement this simple and effective plan. In fact, if you are intelligent enough to put on your socks, you are intelligent enough to follow these instructions thoroughly.

You might wonder where this information came from and why you should believe me—a guy who could put on his socks but wasn't smart enough to change his overloaded schedule. Let me tell you where it came from.

Some time ago, I was able to spend some time with my sister and her husband at their home in California. My brother-in-law had recently retired from his practice as a highly successful physician. He is a brilliant man and did extremely well in medical school. I had two sons in college at the time, and we began talking about their success in school. I mentioned that I wished they were doing a little better. My brother-in-law asked me if I would like to have them become straight-A students. Of course my answer was a resounding yes. He then took the time to tell me about an episode he had during the first part of his medical school experience.

A professor in one of his classes had taken a liking to my brother-in-law and asked him to come into his office. When my brother-in-law arrived, the professor told him that he wanted to share something with him that would help him get straight A's for the rest of his college career. The professor sat him down and outlined the things that I will outline in this book. Following their discussion, my brother-in-law implemented the tools that he had learned and continued from that time to the end of his educational experience to get straight A's.

He subsequently gave this same information to one of his brothers, who was also in school. His brother used it somewhat halfheartedly during his first year and achieved close to a B average. The following year, his brother got more serious about it and implemented the instructions fully. From that time forward, he received straight A's. Several others have also used these techniques and been successful.

You will have the same experience if you will implement these tools as they are presented and follow through in every aspect of the program. The best part is that it will be fun for you to do. What could be more fun than going to a movie or out to dinner the night before the big final exam when your friends and roommates are all sweating it out and cramming as much in as they can? You won't need to cram for tests anymore. You will be able to do whatever you want before the exams because you will be more than ready for them without any extra studying.

One more thing. There are those who think that if you are a straight-A student, you can't be well-rounded or you can't cope with anything other than studying. They think you are a bookworm and don't know how to have a social life. They think you don't know how to have fun and that you must be extremely boring.

But being well-rounded is a result of good study habits and excellent performance in college. It will open so many opportunities for other areas of growth you might not have had otherwise. So don't let the "nerd" factor scare you away from achieving the goal of perfect grades in college. After all, no one needs to know that you are getting straight A's. You can keep that as your little secret (except from your parents if they are paying your way). Of course, when interviewers come to your college to interview students and you happen to be on the top of everyone's lists to hire, it might just slip out that it is because you have straight A's.

With that in mind, let's get this parade going and get you the info you need to have perfect grades.

College, Job—What's the Difference?

There are several reasons for going to college. What's yours? Are you looking for four years of partying? Are you looking for a spouse? Did you just want to get away from home for a few years? Are you on Mom and Dad's four-year vacation plan? Maybe you are looking to really further your education. Maybe you read in the news that college graduates earn several million dollars more in their lifetime than those who only graduate from high school.

So think about it for just a minute. Why are you really going to school? If it's for the social aspect with little care about your grades, give this book to one of your roommates. If, on the other hand, you desire to prepare yourself for the years ahead by obtaining a solid education, then read on.

If you are like most people in college, you are ultimately trying to find your way into a career of some kind. You might be studying chemistry, physics, engineering, medicine, social work, or science. Or you might simply be working on your generals. All of this expense and time is your attempt to prepare yourself for a job. A job is the reward for your efforts while in school. If you are better educated than others in the same job market, the chances are good that you will have an advantage over them in the hiring process.

If you are here in school to prepare for a job, what kind of job are you preparing for? How much time do you expect to spend at your job during a given week? The normal nine-to-five job requires forty hours of time spent at work. If you include some travel time, maybe an hour a day, you will find that you spend a minimum of forty-five hours a week dealing with your job. Of course, you could be spending a lot more than that, but forty-five hours is probably a good average to start with.

Based on that time frame of forty-five hours per week, we are going to treat your school experience like a job. You will need to work roughly the same amount of hours on your schoolwork that you will spend on the job when you get out of school. This is good training. I had a roommate who never spent more than fifteen hours a week on his schoolwork. When he graduated (not with straight A's I might add), he had a terrible time trying to get used to spending forty hours a week involved in one activity. He had not trained himself enough. He lived by the motto that he didn't want his schoolwork to get in the way of his education. Now, I am all for having a great time, especially in college, but there is a time for everything.

So, how are you going to spend job-equivalent time involved in your schoolwork? Here is the first secret.

Secret #1

Spend two hours studying outside of class for every one hour spent in class.

If you take fifteen hours of classes, you will spend thirty hours each week outside of class studying, which will total forty-five hours. It will be just like a job, and the hours you spend will be training you to focus on a specific goal for a sustained period of time. This will prepare you for the effort required by a job better than anything else you could do.

You might think there is not enough time in the day to spend 45 hours or more a week involved in schoolwork. However, there are 168 hours in the week. You will probably spend 56 hours sleeping (8 hours a night), but that still leaves 112 hours for activities. You won't even need to spend half of your time with schoolwork. It will be just a hair over 40 percent. What can you do with the other almost 60 percent of your time? Let's get it all mapped out and organized for you.

Table 1. Take a look at the time chart. Make a copy of this chart or create your own, but don't try to just keep the information for your time chart in your head; you need to write it down. It will only take you about five minutes and a ruler to recreate this chart for yourself. You will need one of these charts for each term or semester.

Your chart should look like this one, starting at 7:00 AM (or earlier if you want) and going to 11:00 PM.

Table 2. First mark on your chart the things that are set in stone—things you cannot change. These are the must-do items like class times. I have used a black background to boldly show that they are unchangeable. You could do them in a specific color to set them apart.

Table 3. The next items that you will want to put on your chart are the things you would like to do. These items could include parties, dates, and sporting events. In my example they have no background color because they are free and easy time.

Table 4. The last things to put on your chart are the study blocks. Be specific not only with your times but also with what you plan to do during those times. *Be sure to block your study times into segments of at least one hour!* Don't try to fit in fifteen minutes here or thirty minutes there; it doesn't work. It takes time to get into your studies and focus on them. If you only have fifteen or thirty minutes, you will barely have enough time to get out your materials and briefly look them over before the time is gone. Remind yourself that you need at least one hour at a time to study. I have marked these study hours with a gray background to show their importance.

You could use a different color for each of the three categories so that it is easy to see on your chart.

*The tables are made up of schedules with five 3-credit hour classes. Note that the classes that meet on Tuesdays and Thursdays go for an hour and a half while the classes that meet on Monday, Wednesday, and Friday are only one hour.

Table 1

	7	8	9	10	11	12	1	2	3	4	5	6	7	8	9	10	11
Sun																	
Mon																	
Tue																	
Wed																	
Thur																	
Fri																	
Sat																	

Table 2

	7	8	9	10	11	12	1	2	3	4	5	6	7	8	9	10	11
Sun						CHURCH											
Mon			MATH	SCI				ENG									
Tue		GEO						MUSIC									
Wed			MATH	SCI				ENG									
Thur		GEO						MUSIC									
Fri			MATH	SCI				ENG									
Sat																	

Table 3

	7	8	9	10	11	12	1	2	3	4	5	6	7	8	9	10	11
Sun					CHURCH												
Mon			MATH	SCI				ENG									
Tue		GEO						MUSIC									
Wed			MATH	SCI				ENG					PARTY				
Thur		GEO						MUSIC									
Fri			MATH	SCI				ENG					DATE NIGHT				
Sat						FOOTBALL GAME							DATE NIGHT				

Table 4

	7	8	9	10	11	12	1	2	3	4	5	6	7	8	9	10	11
Sun					CHURCH												
Mon	STUDY MATH		MATH	SCI	STUDY SCI			ENG	STUDY ENG				STUDY MUSIC				
Tue	STUDY GEO	GEO			STUDY MUSIC			MUSIC					STUDY GEO				
Wed	STUDY MATH		MATH	SCI	STUDY SCI			ENG	STUDY ENG				PARTY				
Thur	STUDY GEO	GEO			STUDY MUSIC			MUSIC					STUDY GEO				
Fri	STUDY MATH		MATH	SCI	STUDY SCI			ENG	STUDY ENG				DATE NIGHT				
Sat						FOOTBALL GAME							DATE NIGHT				

There are advantages to having your chart completed and your time set. First off, notice that there is no study time set up on my chart for either Saturday or Sunday. Your job will hopefully allow you to have these days free to spend with friends and family. With that in mind, I have set it up so you will not need to study on those days.

The second advantage is that you never need to think about what you should be doing at a given time. You know instantly by looking at the chart if you have free time on Thursday at 4:00 PM to take in a matinee at the theater. If something comes up that you really want to do and it is during a mapped out study block, there is a way to do it. Simply move the study block to another open time period. *Make sure you move it and don't just delete it!* If you want to go see a friend in a play on Tuesday evening, go ahead and do it, but move the two study hours you have scheduled to another open two-hour slot later in the week. When the week is over, you want to be sure you spent the two hours doing studies for every hour you spent in class.

The last benefit of mapping things out is

that it gives you an out if something comes up that you really don't want to do. If your friends invite you to go on a blind date with someone that reminds you of one of your grandparents and the thought of going out with the person nauseates you, simply tell your friends that you already have specific plans for that particular time. You can show them your time chart and tell them there is no way you can make the date. Based on some of the blind dates I was forced to go on, this is a good enough reason to set up your time chart.

What Does It Mean to "Double Your Margins"?

Secret #2

Double your margins for notes.

The professor who passed this information on to my brother-in-law told him that almost 90 percent of exam questions are taken from lectures in class. Taking notes properly is vital to the success of the system. Make sure you are meticulous in your note-taking during class.

In your lifetime you have probably taken a lot of notes. You have probably used similar kinds of notepaper for all of those notes. Your standard college-rule paper with a left margin is similar to Notebook Page 1.

Notebook Page 1

That's okay for B-grade work, but for A-grade work you will need to change the margin, making it wider as on Notebook Page 2.

What Does It Mean to "Double Your Margins"?

I have made a new margin line, making the margin twice as wide as it was before. You can do this by putting a straight edge on your paper and drawing a line with your pen.

Notebook Page 2

Now let me explain the reason for the increased margin.

Secret #3

Put pearls of wisdom in the margins of your notes.

What is a pearl of wisdom? Normally you will find that you will have some outside reading or lab work to do for your classes. When you are doing the outside work, you will find little pearls of wisdom that pertain to the notes you have taken in class. When you find one, write it down in the extra-wide margin in the area of your notes where it applies.

For instance, let's say in class your professor describes the four events that allowed Hitler to overpower Poland. Of course you have all four reasons carefully recorded in your notes. Then, when you are studying the reading assignment in the text, you find out there were actually six events that led to Poland's downfall. You would then go to your notes to the point where you had written about the four reasons brought up in class, and in the margin you would note the other two reasons with an arrow pointing to the four reasons in your notes. Look at the following example.

5. No natural boundaries
6. No decent weapons

Hitler was able to overpower Poland for 4 reasons:

1. Poland was not able to prepare for an invasion
2. Some of the Polish people liked Hitler
3. The Polish army was small
4. There were no defences near the border

There are few people who will look things over carefully enough to really see what they are looking at. They look but they do not see and in seeing they still do not understand. This is a frightening concept to realize that most people tread lightly on the surface of life and leave it with little understanding of the importance of really listing.

The true living of life has little to do with waking each morning and wandering about in a daze of repetitive motions. The true art of living exists in taking each day by the horns and riding it for all it is worth. There are few feelings more satisfying and pleasurable than dropping into bed at the end of the day totally exhausted. Not exhausted by the mere dealing with life, but exhausted because of the fulfillment of each moment in the day.

There are few who understand that the larger the island of knowledge, the longer the shoreline of wonder. There will never be enough time in one life to learn everything there is to know, but to suggest that this is a reason not to try at all, would defeat the great purpose of the source from which we came.

Think about the power of this exercise. Other students will simply gloss over the six events, but you will have all six in your notes. When the exam rolls around and one of the questions asks for the events that allowed Hitler to overpower Poland, you will give six events. Even the best of the other students will probably give four. If the professor is grading on a curve, who do you think will get the higher grade? You will, of course!

There is one more thing to say about the pearls of wisdom. If in your reading or lab work you come across something that is interesting but is nowhere to be found in your notes, go ahead and write it in the margin of your notes—but be sure to circle it. By circling it you will know that it is a personal pearl of wisdom. You may never have to use the information from a personal pearl, but it might come in handy if there is an opportunity to expound on a topic in an essay question. In this case, you will have additional material that will put you head and shoulders above the other students.

Let me add that you only need to read the text material once if you do it thoroughly and thoughtfully, making good use of the pearl notes. If you are alert and attentive to what you are reading, you will never have to return to read it again—even just before an exam. This point leads us to the next secret.

Secret #4

Take notes meticulously and use the professor's words and language, not your own.

Sometimes it's easy to take notes by summarizing what the professor has said into your own language and in a style of writing that is similar to shorthand. *It is crucial that you not do this!* You must take notes carefully, consistently, and meticulously, and you must do so in the professor's words.

Certainly everything that is written on the board in class is worthy of finding its way into your notebook just as it is written on the board. Also, there are many points of lecture that don't make it on the board but should be recorded in your notes. Make sure that even these notes are in the words that the professor is using.

Once again, think of the power of this tool. If the professor is looking at two exams or papers and one of them is expressing the ideas in the professor's own words while the other is using the vocabulary and sentence structure of the student, which one do you think will get the most credit? The one who has taken time to relate to the professor on the professor's own terms and in his own language will have the better chance at the higher grade because it makes the professor's job easier; he doesn't have to try to interpret the language of each student to see if the student understood the concept.

If the words coming back to him are his own, he already knows how to interpret them. You have not only saved him time but you have also stopped him from getting a headache, and he will reward you with a higher grade.

A Brief Note on Notes

Secret #5

Read every single note every single day (except Saturday and Sunday).

That means that on day one of the term or semester you will have just a few pages of notes to read from each class. It is important that you read all the notes from each class every day (except for Saturday and Sunday). Set aside a portion of your study blocks for this reading. You can do it during your first study block of the day, a middle study block, or the last one, but be sure to set enough of that study time aside for note reading. You will need to have more time as the term (or semester or quarter) progresses, but don't forget the note reading. It will become one of the most important things you do.

For example, let's say you have a science class on Monday, Wednesday, and Friday. The first day of your science class you take eight pages of notes. You will read those notes during your study time on Monday. You will again read those eight pages of notes on Tuesday even though you don't have science that day. On the second day of class, Wednesday, you take seven additional pages of notes. During your next study time, you will read all fifteen pages of notes for that class. On Thursday you will again read all fifteen pages of notes even though you don't have science on that day either. On the third day of class, Friday, you take another eight pages of notes. On Friday you will read all twenty-three pages of notes from beginning to end. And so it continues throughout the entire quarter, term, or semester and with every single class.

Obviously, by the end of the semester you will be reading a lot of pages of notes every day. It's a good thing you have set aside at least two hours of study time for every hour in class! It might sound crazy to continually read and reread the same notes every day, but the benefits are amazing.

Rereading your notes will actually turn the tables on normal study. Students often go into a test having a sharp memory of their last few days in class and a vague memory of anything beyond a week old. They have tried the week before (or night before) to cram in all of the information from the beginning of the term, but most of it ends up leaking out of one of their ears and onto their shirt collar. Try as they will, they are not able to disperse the heavy cloud that covers their minds and hides most of the old information in a fog. Does this sound familiar? It does to me. I have been there, dirty collars and all, and it is not a comfortable place to be.

Some people possess pure photographic memories and can recall anything they have ever seen. If you have that ability, you probably don't need to read this chapter. (Nice of me to say so when you are at the end of the chapter.) If, on the other hand, you don't have a photographic memory, which most of us don't, you will soon see the benefits of reviewing your notes daily.

After three weeks you will have read the first few pages of notes eighteen times. After four weeks you will have read them twenty-four times, and you will have virtually committed them to memory. You will hear someone bring up a topic in class from a few weeks ago, and you will see in your mind the page your notes for that topic is on because you will get to the point where you can actually visualize your notes.

By the end of the term, you will know the things from the first of the term better than anyone else. You will have almost memorized the notes from the first part of the term and will have a super grasp on the most recent notes as well. Best of all, you will know the notes in your professor's own language and words. That is about as close to having a photographic memory as most of us can come.

Even more, you will have also committed to memory the pearls of wisdom that are in the margins of your notes. They too will become part of your knowledge, and you will amaze your professor by adding additional information to your answers that no one else will even remember. The other students will go over their notes, cramming as well as they can, but few will return to the text material to try to get something out of it. Usually there is too much material and a review of their notes is much easier for them. You, however, have already taken the most pertinent information from the text and inserted it in your notes at the right place.

Once again, what a powerful tool. Your answers will be more complete and your knowledge will be so thorough that your test will shine above the rest. To top it off, you will have recited everything back to your professor in his words and language.

One last benefit is that when you study this way and almost commit your notes to memory, you will retain that information for years to come. It will not leave you the day after the exam. Instead, it will contribute to your general store of knowledge and help you in many facets of your life (like winning at trivia games).

The other students will lose most of what they have crammed into their minds because they did not take the time to prepare the soil of the mind for the harvest. You have plowed the field, treated the soil, planted the seeds, and watered the field in order to have a bounteous harvest at exam time. The other students have tried to plow, prepare, plant, water, and harvest all within the same day, and it simply cannot be done. In order to reap the entire harvest, you have to have taken the time from the beginning of the season to accomplish the task.

This Is Only a Test

Secret #6

Outline the entire answer to an exam question on the first page of your answer sheets. Follow your outline with precision as you expand your answer.

Most students almost writhe in pain at the thought of an essay exam. Because they don't know the material, they hope for a multiple choice test that will give them a chance to guess the correct answer. An essay exam reveals what you know (and don't know) about a subject. Multiple choice can reveal that you are good at guessing through the process of elimination. I'll bet that the student who answered the following question wishes that it had been multiple choice.

3. Find x.

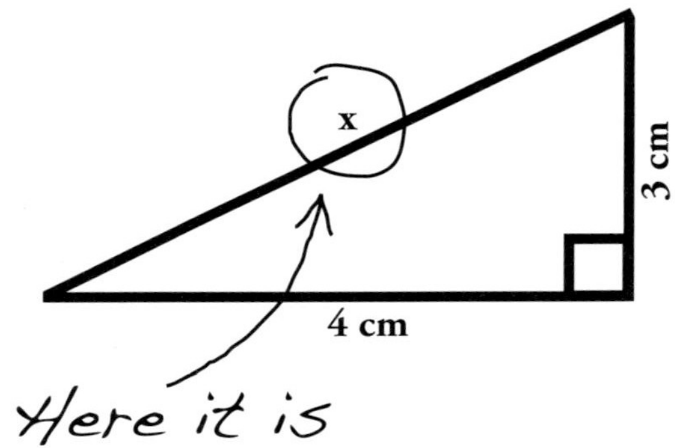

This is an actual answer on a test! Amazing that the student wasn't embarrassed enough by his lack of knowledge to not put anything instead of this. So much for being too brief in an essay answer.

Here is another example of someone who didn't know the material but wanted to try to fill up some empty space with something relevant. That goal is not quite met and the answer is marked incorrect.

Graph of overall mass vs. time

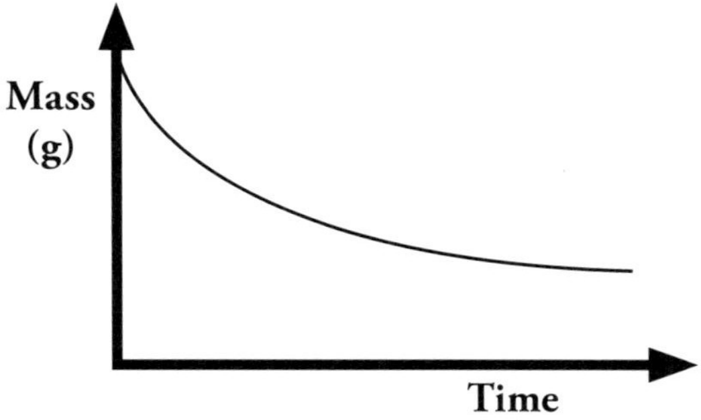

1. Explain the slope of the graph.

It's curvy, with a higher bit at the end and a rather aestehtically pleasing slope downward toward a pretty flat, straight bit. The actual graph itself consists of 2 straight lines meeting at the lower left hand corner of the graph and moving away at a 90 degree angle. Each line has an arrowhead on the end.

Some students think that if they over expound with incorrect information, the professor will mistake their verbosity for knowledge. They think that essay exams are great because they can put enough words on the paper to get some credit. Here is another actual example of a student's paper. I think Jeremy must have experienced a little bit of brain El Niño.

Jeremy, PLEASE, a little less drama!

Jeremy Student

El Niño is spanish. It is the word for child. Like all things Spanish, it is dangerous. It kills people and burns down trees. This child is more than a child. It really isn't a child at all. It is a storm. A deadly storm that kills people and burns down trees.

Warm water usually builds up around Austraila. But not anymore. El Niño moves warm water from Australia to somewhere else, namely to other places. Where are these other places? These are places that also have water, but water that is usualy not as warm as the warm water El Niño moves to these said other places. These places are to the east. Of the water.

In Peru, they have many names for many thirgs. One of the things they have names for is for people who go fishing to make a living. If we had a word for this kind of people, that word would be "fisherman." But we don't. In Peru they have different names for things than we do in America. They call that kind of people "pescadores." That's Sparish. That's what they speak in Peru. When El Niño comes, these "pes-cadores" can't catch any fish. El Niño is caused when the Peruvian gods get angry. They have been angry for millions of years and have made El Niño for millions of years.

Many many moons ago, the Peruvians commtted human sacrifice to satiate their gods and end the flood that was caused by El Niño. In today's modern dog-eat-dog world of scientists, dimplomats, McSalad Shakers, and George Bush Jr., we no longer have access to such solutions We are too proud. We will not commit human sacrifices. We refuse to satiate the Peruvian gods. Thus, they remain angry and keep killing us and burning down our trees with El Niño. Many of these "scientists" have tried to control El Niño with "sci-ence." They put up expensive fish-attracting-bueys that run on flashlight batteries. Imagine fighting the power of the gods with flashlight batteries! Needless to say, this didn't work and everyone died.

When you have an exam coming, you won't be like these other students; you will hope it is an essay exam. An essay exam will give you the opportunity to showcase your knowledge of the topic. You will shine like a 500-watt lightbulb in a room full of candles.

Here is how to do it. We have already discussed that by the time the test shows up, you will have read and reread your notes until you have the material down cold. You will not only know the things that were given in the class notes, but you will also have the pearls of wisdom in your margins committed to memory. On top of all that, you will have reviewed all your notes in your professor's own language and words. What an opportunity to spit out your wealth of knowledge on paper and to style your answer in the right language.

Now the nuts and bolts. On the first page of the answer (normally you will be given several pages to answer an essay question) outline your answer completely. For example, if the question were something like "Explain the events that led to the fall of Poland into Hitler's hands," you would outline your answer by putting the four incidents discussed in class labeled 1 through 4.

You would also add the two pearls of wisdom that you found in your text reading as numbers 5 and 6. Following these items, you could put something brief about each one and include something that you had circled in your notes as interesting but not necessarily crucial to the fall of Poland. Put all of this brief information on the first page.

Then answer the question in great detail beginning on the second page. Be certain to follow your outline meticulously. Don't change the order of the items, and make sure you include everything that is on your outline in your detailed answer. If you remember something important that is not in your outline while you are expanding your answer, go back to your outline and add the new idea right where you are going to put it in your answer. It is important your outline and your expanded answer match up perfectly without any missing parts or conflicts.

The reason they must match up perfectly is simple. When the professor is reading your answers, he might see the outline and think, "This student doesn't know very much about the question. He has the basic points but not the meat of the answer." When he turns to the second page, he will begin to read the expansion of your answer and will be very impressed with your knowledge and how you have expressed the answer in *his words*.

In his mind, he will compare the expanded answer with the outline answer and see they are perfectly aligned. Your first answer will give the professor a heads-up on the next one. He will look at the outline and know that there is more to your answer. He will turn the page and read the expanded answer and be impressed again with your knowledge. If the professor is in a hurry or doesn't want to spend time reading your expanded answers, he can go through your outlines knowing that your answers are complete, detailed, and correct. You will get brownie points for saving him time.

There could be another benefit of doing it this way. When my brother-in-law was taking a test in college, he had made his careful outlines and had been expounding on them thoroughly.

But time ran out, and he only had a few minutes to answer the last question. He was only able to put together the outline. He had no time to even begin the expansion of his answer.

When the professor was grading the exams, he noticed that my brother-in-law had not done the expansion on the last question. However, because he had seen the pattern of knowledge my brother-in-law displayed in the previous questions, he knew that my brother-in-law knew the answer based on his outline. The professor gave him full credit on the question. Now, that might not happen every time you take an exam, but it couldn't hurt to follow the procedure, just in case.

I hope none of you are thinking, "Hey, I can put down the outline and the expansion for the first two or three questions, and then I can just put a bunch of garbage for the expansion information because the professor probably won't read it anyway." If that thought ran through your mind, give yourself a good, solid slap. Remember that this is your opportunity to demonstrate your knowledge. By the time of the exam, you have already done your preparatory work. Just follow the directions and you will do great!

Cram It? No Thanks, No Need!

Let's talk briefly about the benefits of this program. First, you will see more A's on your tests and papers than you will see on the Oakland Athletics bench—*if* you carefully follow the steps outlined in this book. You can't help but do better in college (unless of course you are a genius or you are majoring in bowling).

Your confidence will increase because of your grades. When recruiters come to your college or university, you will be anxious to talk to them because you can tell them about your great grades. You will also be able to answer almost any questions about your specific field of study because you have been practically memorizing the notes you took in class. You will be an impressive interview.

You will also benefit more in the long run

because your knowledge will be permanent in your mind. Those who cram everything in at the last minute have a fairly short retention rate because of the immediate overload. You, on the other hand, will retain your knowledge for many years to come. You will even be able to remember where on the note page the information was written. You will be great at trivia games and word games. Your social skills will improve because you will be able to talk intelligently on a variety of subjects.

Another great benefit is that you will be able to relax the day or week before an exam. Others will be up late trying to cram for it, and you will be able to take in some rays by the pool or go to a movie. You can even make fun of your roommates because they will have to cram and you won't. You can even tell them that they can cram all they want but you will still outperform them on the test. Then you can carefully watch your back because, surely, at least one of them will seek revenge! Maybe you just better keep it to the movies or by the pool in silence.

Also remember that smart people (smart meaning the amount of knowledge someone has) tend to do better in life than those who are not. Your chances of being more successful in whatever you decide to do are increased by the intelligence you have and the grades you have received. You will find yourself acting in a positive way. You will look at the thirty-two-ounce glass with sixteen ounces of water in it and not only say it is half full, but you will also find a way to get another sixteen ounces into it! When your attitude is positive, virtually nothing can stop you in accomplishing your goals.

Plus, your parents will not be upset at you for wasting their money to send you to school. Even more, if they aren't paying your way, you won't be upset at yourself for wasting *your* money to go to school. The list of benefits could go on for a long time. Just know that it will change your life for the better and forever.

The Guarantee

If you follow every tool in this book carefully and completely, you will be guaranteed to get straight A's. The exception to that is if you are in a class that grades on a curve and there are only a few students in the class. My brother had an upper level class that was graded on a curve, and even though he had 98.5 percent for his cumulative percentage, he received a B because there was one other student whose average was above his. So I cannot guarantee that you will get straight A's in such an environment where the curve is used.

However, if you follow the tools precisely and can show that you have followed them by sending me your time schedules, class notes, and so forth, I will refund the money you spent on the book minus a restocking fee if the book is in acceptable condition. The bottom line is that you will be doing much better in your classes if you follow this information.

Of course, I could guarantee that you will get straight A's on your grade report and then offer to fix any A's that are printed crooked.

Let me mention that there might be times at the beginning of the semester or term when there just aren't two hours of work to do for the hour you spent in class. There will be some lulls when you are thinking, "What can I do? I have read the text, covered my notes, and thought of every angle of the lecture I possibly can, and I still have an hour to spend on studying for this class. I know that I am getting an A in this class and there is nothing more I can study today that will be of any help to me."

If that does happen to you, which it probably will, don't worry. The first thing to do is to think about your other classes. Would it help you to spend some of your extra time you had planned for your health class in studying math? If you are on top of all of your classes and you have done everything for that particular class you can think of, take a break, *but don't get in the habit!* You will definitely need to spend the two hours out for each hour in just after a few class periods. Don't give up. Your straight A's are right around the corner.

About the Author

Lyman Hinckley Rose was born in Salt Lake City, Utah, to Ford Thomas Rose and Beulah Hinckley Rose. He served as a missionary for The Church of Jesus Christ of Latter-day Saints for two years in Sydney, Australia. After his mission, Lyman graduated from Brigham Young University in 1985 with a degree in business finance. He then worked for his father's business and later opened his own business as a marketing consultant.

Lyman married the former Lesa Peterson in 1982. They have nine children and are currently living in Bountiful, Utah. The Rose family enjoys camping, traveling, fishing, riding motorcycles, and playing sports. Lyman is also the author of *Dare to Prepare*, *The Lord Kneads You*, *Pure and Chased*, and *Winning the War Against Debt*.

0 26575 50923 6